Piano Exam Pieces

ABRSM Grade 7

Selected from the 2017 & 2018 syllabus

Name

Date of e:

Contents

Editor for ABRSM: Richard Jones

Other pieces for Grade 7

First published in 2016 by ABRSM (Publishing) Ltd,
a wholly owned subsidiary of ABRSM, 24 Portland Place,
London W1B 1LU, United Kingdom
© 2016 by The Associated Board of the Royal Schools of Music
Distributed worldwide by Oxford University Press

Music origination by Julia Bovee
Cover by Kate Benjamin & Andy Potts
Printed in England by Caligraving Ltd, Thetford,
Norfolk, on materials from sustainable sources.

Allegro assai

Second movement from Sonata in G, Op. 1 No. 2

Muzio Clementi
(1752–1832)

Muzio Clementi, an English composer of Italian birth, settled in London in 1774 and established a successful career as a pianist and teacher. His most important compositions are his keyboard works, which include about 70 solo sonatas as well as sonatinas and variations. During a continental tour as a solo pianist in the early 1780s, he stayed in Vienna for six months, taking part in a famous piano contest with Mozart. Afterwards, Mozart commented on his 'remarkable technique at the keyboard'. In 1798 Clementi established a firm in London that not only published music but also manufactured pianos.

Clementi's Six Sonatas, Op. 1, appeared in *c.*1771 during an early period of seven or eight years (*c.*1766–74) in which he was studying music and acting as house musician at the Dorset country estate of Peter Beckford, to whom the sonatas are dedicated. The finale of Sonata No. 2 in G, selected here, was borrowed from an unpublished sonata in the same key (WoO 14) that dates from 1768, when the composer was only 17. It displays an early Classical style, with the occasional hint of Domenico Scarlatti. The piece falls into rondo form – A (upbeat to b. 1), B (b. 21), A (upbeat to b. 63), C (b. 83), A (upbeat to b. 133) – though with elements of binary-sonata form: A + B make up a tonic-dominant exposition, but the tonic-minor episode C replaces a development section, and only A is recapitulated at the end. Grace-notes are to be played on the beat (all slurs to grace-notes are editorial).

Source: *Six Sonatas for the Harpsichord or Piano Forte*, Op. 1 (London: Welcker, 1771)

Please turn the page for the music.

Presto

Third movement from Sonata in F, Hob. XVI:23

Edited by Howard Ferguson

Joseph Haydn
(1732–1809)

Haydn's reputation has long rested largely on his symphonies and string quartets, but it is now widely recognized that his piano sonatas are of comparable importance. He composed over 60 sonatas during a period of roughly 35 years (c.1761–95).

Between 1774 and 1780 Haydn published three sets of six sonatas, which occupy a transitional place between his earlier *Sturm und Drang* (Storm and Stress) sonatas and the Classical-style sonatas of 1783–95. The first set was composed in 1773 and published shortly afterwards (Vienna, 1774) with a dedication to Haydn's employer, Prince Nikolaus Esterházy. It is the Presto-finale from the third of these sonatas that is selected here. A monothematic sonata-form movement, it is largely dominated by the typically graceful opening subject, of which a variant forms the second subject in the dominant key (b. 33). Note the 'comical differences in articulation between [its entries in] bb. 33, 35 and 41' (Howard Ferguson). Further variation of this theme occurs in the development (upbeat to b. 53), largely in related minor keys. In this section, bb. 68–73 might be played with *tenuto* touch, as if notated | ♪ . ♪ . ♪ | etc. The recapitulation (b. 94) is first expanded (bb. 99–111 are new) and then condensed (the material from bb. 14–21 is omitted), with characteristic Haydnesque freedom.

Sources: autograph MS, Sonata No. 3 from *Sei Sonate per Cembalo*, 1773 (Paris, Bibliothèque nationale); first edition, Sonata No. 3 from *Sei Sonate da Clavicembalo* (Vienna: Kurzböck, 1774)

Sonata in B minor

Kp. 377

Domenico Scarlatti
(1685–1757)

Domenico Scarlatti, son of the celebrated Neapolitan opera composer Alessandro, emigrated to Portugal in 1719 and then to Spain in 1728. He spent the rest of his life in Madrid as *maestro de capilla* and music master to the young Princess Maria Barbara, who later became Queen of Spain. Most of his solo keyboard sonatas, well over 500 in number, were composed after his emigration to the Iberian peninsula.

Scarlatti's own description of his sonatas in the preface to the *Essercizi* of 1738, the only collection he published himself, applies equally to later pieces such as this B minor Sonata: 'In these compositions, do not expect any profound learning, but rather an ingenious jesting with art.'

Since there are no dynamics in the source, their choice is left to the player's discretion. Scarlatti's mature binary form is a clear precursor of Classical sonata form. In this sonata, a first group, rich in ideas, includes written-out trills over an ostinato bass (bb. 8 and 10), repeated notes plus decorative trill figures (bb. 13–14), octaves plus descending 4th figures (b. 24), and a variant of the same, with the octaves in rhythmic augmentation (b. 30). The second subject (b. 34), in the relative major D, forms a complete contrast – more lyrical, and characterized by the syncopated rhythms and appoggiatura cadences of the *galant* style that swept Europe in the mid-18th century. After a brief modulatory development (b. 48), the tonic return (b. 63) coincides with a partial recapitulation of the first group, now in a different order. Finally, the second subject returns (b. 75), transposed to the tonic B minor.

Source: Parma MSS, Vol. X, No. 20

14

Nocturne in C sharp minor

Op. posth., KK IVa, No. 16

Fryderyk Chopin
(1810–49)

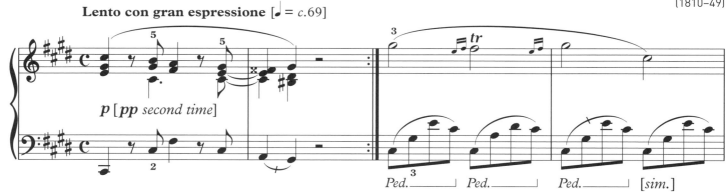

The title 'nocturne' was first used by the Irish pianist-composer John Field in the early-19th century to describe a lyrical, song-like piano piece, with pedalled broken-chordal accompaniment, that evokes a dreamy, night-time atmosphere. The high point of the genre was reached in the 21 surviving nocturnes by the Polish pianist-composer Fryderyk Chopin. The majority of these pieces were composed after Chopin had settled in Paris in 1831, but several early nocturnes, including this piece, were composed before he left Warsaw in November 1830 at the age of 20, and remained unpublished during his lifetime.

The early Nocturne in C sharp minor was composed in the spring of 1830 and dedicated to Chopin's sister Ludwika. It is cast in a simple ternary form, ABA[1] (bb. 3, 19 and 44). The B-section (b. 19), which begins in the submediant A major, quotes from Chopin's F minor piano concerto, which was premiered by the composer in March 1830 – around the time when the nocturne was composed. This Nocturne is heard at the beginning and the end of Roman Polanski's 2002 film *The Pianist*.

Sources: Polish first edition (Poznań: M. Leitgeber, 1875); English first edition (London: E. Ascherberg, 1894).

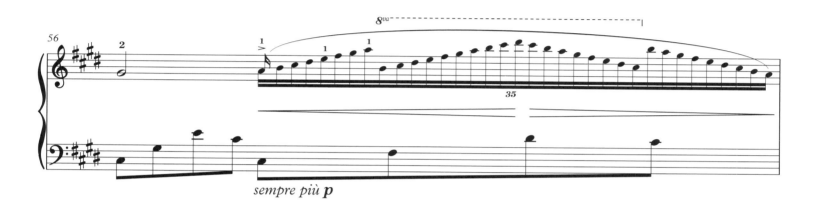

情歌 Qing Ge

Love Song

No. 1 from Two Folksongs

Wanghua Chu
(born 1941)

Moderato andante [♩ = c.40]

Wanghua Chu studied piano and composition at the Central Conservatory of Music in Beijing, where he was later appointed a lecturer. In the late 1980s he undertook postgraduate studies at the University of Melbourne, Australia. He is best known for his successful amalgamation of Chinese and Western musical styles in his piano works.

'Love Song', the first of Two Folksongs (民歌两首 Min Ge Liang Shou), is a traditional melody from Kangding in the Sichuan province of China. The whole tune is played twice (bb. 3 and 18) – second time, with a richer texture and varied harmonization. Note the left-hand echoes at the phrase ends in bb. 6 and 10. The last phrase (b. 11) is varied three times at the end (bb. 26, 31 and 36), bringing the piece to a powerful and heartfelt conclusion.

Summer Song

Sommervise

No. 3 from *Fantasistykker*, Op. 45

B:3

Agathe Backer Grøndahl
(1847–1907)

Andantino semplice ♩ = 104

The Norwegian composer and pianist Agathe Backer Grøndahl studied with Bülow in Florence and with Liszt in Weimar. She toured as a concert pianist in Scandinavia, Germany and England, earning a reputation as an outstanding player. She is best known today as a composer of songs, Norwegian folksong arrangements, and piano pieces – mostly lyrical, with descriptive titles, and often with considerable melodic charm.

'Sommervise', from *Fantasistykker* (Fantasy Pieces), Op. 45, is cast in a simple bipartite form with varied repeats (A: bb. 1 and 9; B: bb. 17 and 25). The repeats are varied by moving the melody to the left hand and accompanying it in the right hand with decorative, impressionistic trill figures.

Source: *Fantasistykker*, Op. 45 (Oslo, 1897)

Waltz

Valse

No. 5 from *Valses nobles et sentimentales*

C:1

Maurice Ravel
(1875–1937)

Presque lent – dans un sentiment intime [quite slow – with an intimate feeling] ♩ = 96

le chant très en dehors [melody very prominent]

Maurice Ravel was born in the Basque region of France, but his family moved to Paris when he was only one year old. He became a pupil of Fauré at the Paris Conservatoire, but was equally influenced by Chabrier and by Liszt, whose virtuoso piano writing he was to surpass (though no great pianist himself) in some of his larger works. He was a master of subtle, brilliant orchestration, with a highly individual harmonic idiom.

Ravel's *Valses nobles et sentimentales* (Noble and Sentimental Waltzes) are prefaced by a quotation from Henri de Régnier: 'the delicious and ever-new pleasure of a useless occupation'. The eight pieces were first performed in 1911, and in the following year they were orchestrated by the composer and transformed into a ballet, *Adélaïde, ou Le langage des fleurs* (Adelaide, or the Language of Flowers). Ravel's instruction in bb. 19–20 applies to the dotted crotchets.

Source: *Valses nobles et sentimentales* (Paris: Durand, 1911)

la partie supérieure en dehors [top part prominent]

C:2

Forcing the Pace

No. 7 from *Rock Preludes 2*

Christopher Norton
(born 1953)

Christopher Norton is a British pianist and composer who was born in New Zealand and completed an honours music degree at Otago University, Dunedin, in 1974. He emigrated to Britain in 1977 and studied composition with Wilfred Mellers and David Blake at York University. Norton composes in a variety of contemporary popular styles. *Microjazz*, begun in 1983, has become a successful and widely used educational series.

Norton's rock prelude *Forcing the Pace* is essentially bipartite: an exposition, consisting of themes A (b. 1) and B (b. 9) plus episode C (b. 25), is followed by a reprise (A at b. 35, B at b. 59), interrupted by a new episode D (b. 43) and brought to a conclusion by a coda (b. 77). A more moderate tempo than the composer's indicated above – perhaps ♩ = *c*.166 – would be acceptable in the exam.

Humoresque

No. 3 from Humoresques, Op. 126

Jean Absil
(1893–1974)

The Belgian composer Jean Absil studied at the Brussels Conservatory from 1913 with a view to pursuing a career as an organist, and then again in 1920–2, this time setting his sights on becoming a composer. He began teaching at the same conservatory in 1930 and was later a professor there for 20 years (1939–59). His mature, polytonal style was influenced by Berg, Milhaud, Hindemith and others.

Absil inherited from Schumann, Dvořák and other 19th-century composers his use of the title 'humoresque' for a fanciful piece that conveyed a certain 'humour', or state of mind – not necessarily wit, though this particular piece is full of it! Toccata-like in manner, it falls into a tripartite form: A (upbeat to b. 1), B (b. 23), A (b. 42), plus coda (based on B; b. 63). The musical material includes a comic, syncopated theme over cross-rhythm ostinato (b. 2), contrary-motion chromatics (b. 11), and dissonant chords in a subversive rhythm, reminiscent of Stravinsky or Bartók (first at b. 23; fully developed at bb. 40 and 63).

Source: *Humoresques*, Op. 126 (Paris: Lemoine, 1966)